NBA SLAM

BY JOHN HAREAS

SCHOLASTIC INC.

New York   Toronto   London   Auckland   Sydney

Mexico City   New Delhi   Hong Kong

To my two favorite All-Stars,
Jennifer and Emma
—J.H.

PHOTO CREDITS:
NBA Photos
Cover (Bryant), 21: Fernando Medina. **Cover (Carter), 22:** Nathaniel S. Butler. **Cover (Webber):** Garrett Ellwood.
Cover (Garnett), 16: David Sherman. **Back Cover (Finley), 3, 5, 7, 10, 11, 17, 19, 23, 27, 28, 30, 31, 32:** Andrew D. Bernstein.
6, 25: Rocky Widner. **8:** Noren Trotman. **9:** Bill Baptist. **12:** Lou Cappozzola. **13:** Steve Woltman. **14:** Steve DiPaola.
15: Glenn James. **18:** Layne Murdoch. **20:** Jon Hayt. **24:** Jeff Vinick. **26:** NBA Photo Library. **29:** Walter Iooss.

Footage courtesy of NBA Entertainment. Video Stills by Steven Freeman. Special thanks to Joe Amati of NBA Photos;
Charles Rosenzweig, Steve Howser and Michael Levine of NBA Entertainment; Paul Zeise and Adam Kamins of
NBA Publishing Ventures; Bethany Buck and Erin Soderberg at Scholastic Inc.

ISBN 0-439-14070-6

© 2000 by NBA Properties, Inc.
All rights reserved. Published by Scholastic Inc.

12 11 10 9 8 7 6 5 4 3 2   0 1 2 3 4 5/0

Printed in the U.S.A.
First Scholastic printing, February 2000
Book design: Michael Malone

Finesse versus POWER

There are two styles of dunking in the game of basketball. One involves graceful moves that are flashy and ballet-like. Players who dunk this way are called "Sky Walkers." Sky Walkers don't just glide to the hoop; they hang in midair and change direction before delivering the ball to the basket. They possess a flair for the dramatic. They are the ultimate showmen.

The NBA's top aerial acrobats include Kobe Bryant of the Los Angeles Lakers, Vince Carter of the Toronto Raptors, Michael Finley of the Dallas Mavericks, Larry Hughes of the Philadelphia 76ers and Antonio McDyess of the Denver Nuggets.

The other dunking style is much more definitive. It's a demonstration of power. Pure power. "Power Dunkers" dunk the ball with tremendous force, using their size and brute strength to muscle under the basket. These players are less concerned with style points and more concerned with intimidating their opponents. "You can't stop me, and to prove it, I'm going to dunk on you," is more like their mentality.

MICHAEL FINLEY

The NBA's premier Power Dunkers are Kevin Garnett of the Minnesota Timberwolves, Shawn Kemp of the Cleveland Cavaliers, Alonzo Mourning of the Miami Heat, Shaquille O'Neal of the Los Angeles Lakers and Chris Webber of the Sacramento Kings.

Both the Sky Walkers and the Power Dunkers must pay their respects to the founding fathers of dunk. Elgin Baylor, Connie Hawkins and Julius Erving were the original princes of midair, dazzling crowds with their above-the-rim play. Wilt Chamberlain, Gus Johnson and Darryl Dawkins were among the power dunking pioneers who intimidated opponents with their thunderous slams.

Players such as Dominique Wilkins, Michael Jordan and Shawn Kemp also made their mark in the NBA Slam Dunk contest, which showcased the league's finest dunkers at All-Star Weekend from 1984 to 1997. After a two-year hiatus, the Slam Dunk contest is back. But you don't have to wait for February to roll around to view awesome jams—you can see your favorite dunkers during the regular season. If you're lucky enough to see one of these players in person, you'll experience firsthand the eruption in the arena after a mammoth jam.

Regardless of style—finesse or power—the end result is the same. The dunk is worth two points whether it's a 360-degree slam or a monster jam on a player's head. Either way, the move is explosive and exciting and causes pandemonium in the arena.

Read on for a celebration of basketball's most electrifying play and the NBA's top dunkers, past and present.

KOBE BRYANT

KOBE
BRYANT

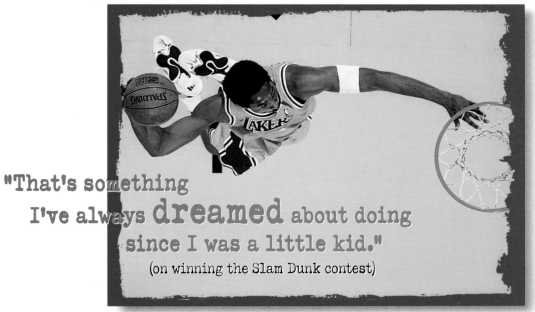

"That's something I've always dreamed about doing since I was a little kid."

(on winning the Slam Dunk contest)

Kobe's coming-out party was held in Cleveland during the 1997 NBA All-Star Weekend. It was a cold February night when he showcased to the world his repertoire of imaginative dunks. Kobe dazzled fans in the NBA All-Star Slam Dunk contest with one spectacular move after another. His first dunk was a powerful reverse jam that had 20,000 fans roaring with approval. Then, in the finals, Kobe literally flexed his muscles when he ran to the hoop, brought the ball between his legs and used a windmill slam to seal the deal. Afterward, Kobe flexed his biceps after clinching first place.

"I know I don't have much," he says. "But I decided to flex what I have."

Ever since then, Kobe has muscled his way to the top to become one of the NBA's premier dunkers. Alley-oops, tip-in slams, breakaway jams—you name it and Kobe has it—a flair for all the most spectacular moves. And with an off-the-charts leaping ability, who could blame him for wanting to show off his mad hops?

DID YOU KNOW? KOBE BECAME THE YOUNGEST PLAYER EVER TO START IN AN ALL-STAR GAME WHEN HE TOOK THE FLOOR FOR THE 1998 WESTERN CONFERENCE ALL-STAR TEAM AT AGE 19.

VINCE CARTER

"I like **stylin'**. I'm starting to allow my **spontaneous** side to come out."

The comparisons began the moment Vince Carter started playing. Not even one month into his NBA career, Vince had already been likened to some of the NBA's all-time great players. Michael Jordan. Dr. J. Dominique Wilkins. Basketball legends and dunking machines.

With explosive hops that translate into a 41-inch vertical leap and a flair for the dramatic, it's easy to see why so many people are climbing aboard the Vince Carter bandwagon.

"I'm an emotional, energetic person," says Vince. "I want to bring a different aspect to the game for the fans to enjoy."

From one continent to another, fans are in awe of Carter's showstopping, gravity-defying dunks: Tomahawk. Windmill. Turnaround. Three-sixty.

"He's the best dunker I've ever seen," says former North Carolina Coach Dean Smith, who coached Jordan as well as Carter. And speaking of Jordan, how does Vince feel about his style of game being compared to one of the game's all-time great players?

"It's a great honor to be placed in Michael's company, but I want to put my name on the map with what I can do."

DID YOU KNOW? VINCE AND TORONTO RAPTORS TEAMMATE TRACY MCGRADY ARE COUSINS.

MICHAEL
FINLEY

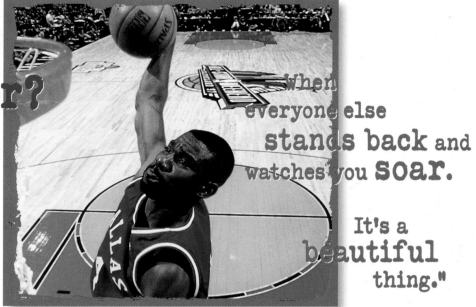

"How do you know you've arrived as a **dunker?** When everyone else **stands back** and watches you **soar.** It's a **beautiful thing.**"

Some players perfect the dunk at local playgrounds, spending hours upon hours practicing their timing and hand—eye coordination. For Michael Finley of the Dallas Mavericks, the bedroom served as his personal launching pad.

"My first dunks were in the dirty clothes hamper," says Finley. From dirty socks to grass-stained pants, nothing was sacred in the Finley household when it came to flying to the hoop, er, hamper. "I made the first dunk I ever tried and kept dunking regularly without ever missing—at least until I went outside."

Finley's devotion in grade school paid off at the high school level where he dunked for the very first time on a real basket. He quickly earned bragging rights on campus, wowing his classmates with his ability to sky.

Now in his fifth NBA season, Finley can boast as one of the game's most creative and explosive dunkers. He can slam two balls on one dunk. He can also pass the ball to himself, do a cartwheel and then jam it home. Wow! He's certainly come a long way from his hamper.

DID YOU KNOW? IN HIGH SCHOOL, MICHAEL WON A CHANCE THROUGH A LOCAL CHICAGO TELEVISION STATION TO PLAY ONE-ON-ONE WITH HIS BOY-HOOD IDOL MICHAEL JORDAN.

LARRY
HUGHES

"It feels good to hear the crowd after a dunk.

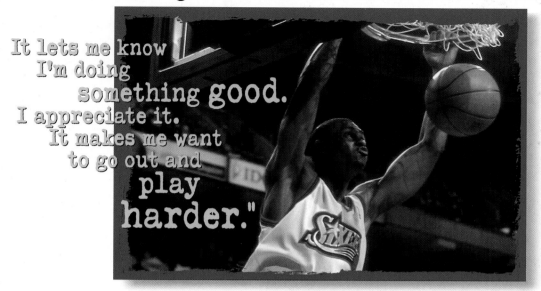

It lets me know
I'm doing
something good.
I appreciate it.
It makes me want
to go out and
play
harder."

He is not as well known as his celebrated backcourtmate, Allen Iverson, but give Larry Hughes time. The 6–5 guard electrifies crowds with breathtaking leaping ability that has caused quite a stir around the league. He and Iverson equal athleticism, excitement and trouble for Sixers opponents. They already form one of the best alley-oop tandems in the NBA. Some of their recent highlights go like this: *Iverson steals the ball and sprints down the court, sees Hughes alongside him, and lobs a soft pass high above the glass to the second-year guard—ka-boom! It's an easy two. Talk about redefining hang time! Hughes was up there a long time.*

Hughes isn't just an offensive highlight film, though. He's also an excellent defender. Larry's knack for stripping the ball from his opponent only means another clear departure for Philadelphia Flight Number 21. See, when Larry dunks, whether it's an alley-oop, one-handed slam or reverse, one thing is certain—no matter the move, he leaves his opponents earthbound.

DID YOU KNOW? LARRY WAS THE ONLY PLAYER OUT OF THE TOP 10 SELECTIONS IN THE 1998 NBA DRAFT TO ADVANCE INTO THE SECOND ROUND OF THE 1999 NBA PLAYOFFS. LARRY WAS SELECTED EIGHTH OVERALL.

ANTONIO
McDYESS

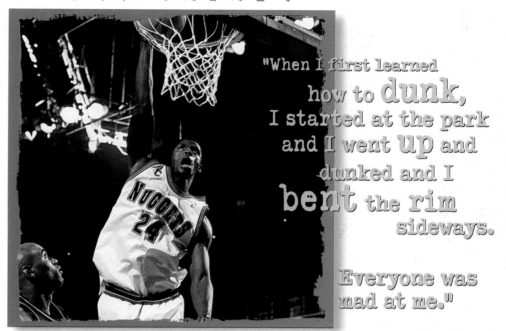

"When I first learned how to **dunk,** I started at the park and I went **up** and dunked and I **bent** the **rim** sideways.

Everyone was mad at me."

He is only 25 years old and the stories of his leaping ability are already legendary. To say Antonio McDyess has hops doesn't quite do him justice. When you can leave palm prints high on the backboard glass, you have mad hops. And Antonio McDyess has mad hops.

McDyess, with his 42-inch vertical leap, routinely leaps over opponents, throwing down one spectacular dunk after another. He'll dunk through opponents and he'll dunk over opponents; it doesn't matter. As a power forward, McDyess isn't supposed to make crowds ooh and aah with his leaping ability. After all, power forwards are supposed to be big and bulky, taking up lots of space under the basket. They're not supposed to have the flair for the midair.

But McDyess isn't your typical power forward. His long arms and springlike legs allow him to take flight more quickly than his counterparts. Luckily, the thin air in Denver doesn't make Antonio jump any higher. If it did, someone would definitely have to raise the baskets.

DID YOU KNOW? ANTONIO BLOCKED SIX SHOTS IN A GAME AGAINST SAN ANTONIO IN ONLY HIS SECOND SEASON.

KEVIN GARNETT

"Sometimes I'm **zoned out** and I don't see nothing but the **hoop** and **watch out!**

Here I come!"

Don't let the skinny frame fool you. K.G. may not look as imposing as Shaquille O'Neal or Alonzo Mourning, but the 6–11 forward can throw down the rock with the best of them. At 220 pounds, one would think that K.G. would get pushed around, especially by bodies weighing well over 70 pounds more than him! Rather, Garnett does the punishing, thanks to the agility and coordination that make him a virtual pogo stick around the hoop.

Nicknamed "Da Kid" when he entered the NBA, Garnett quickly earned the respect of his peers by making the All-Star team in only his second season. K.G. soon elevated his status to Da Man with his play and his ability to rock the house with his dunking ability.

Garnett is a showman. When he dunks, he wants to impress the fans in the arena. "I'm an emotional player," says Garnett. "I play off the crowd."

His game may be finesse, but ask any number of players who have experienced a K.G. special and they'll tell you: Da Man has got Da goods.

DID YOU KNOW? AS A MEMBER OF THE 2000 U.S. MEN'S OLYMPIC TEAM, GARNETT FINISHED FOURTH OR BETTER ON TEAM U.S.A. IN POINTS, REBOUNDS, ASSISTS, BLOCKS AND STEALS DURING THE 1999 PRE-OLYMPIC QUALIFYING TOURNAMENT.

"I get **excited** after a dunk, I **yell** and **scream**, but it's not yelling and screaming at other players to show them up.

What I do is have **fun** on **the court.**"

Shawn Kemp doesn't just dunk the ball, he power slams it through the hoop. He is known to jam with such force that in high school, he once caught a ball in midair, spun 360 degrees and threw it down. What's the big deal? Sparks flew off the metal-chained net!

Kemp has been electrifying NBA fans with an array of dazzling jams throughout his 10-year career. It was his participation in the NBA's Slam Dunk contests that made him a household name. With powerful legs and a thick, sculpted upper body, Kemp impressed fans with a variety of tomahawks and windmills.

Kemp quickly earned the nickname "Reign Man" when he played for the Seattle SuperSonics, because he dominates on the court and, just like rain, showers opponents with driving slams. Now a member of the Cleveland Cavaliers, the nickname is still appropriate. No one has figured out how to stop the Reign.

DID YOU KNOW? SHAWN HAS PARTICIPATED IN FOUR NBA SLAM DUNK CONTESTS IN HIS CAREER. HIS HIGHEST FINISH CAME IN 1991, WHEN HE WAS RUNNER-UP TO DEE BROWN.

ALONZO MOURNING

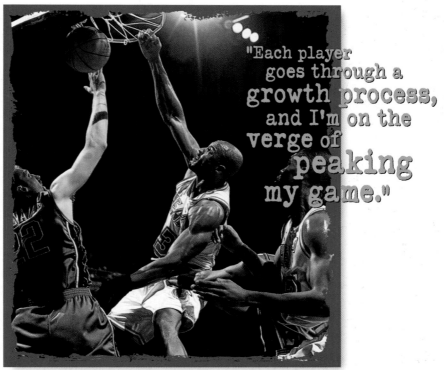

"Each player goes through a **growth process**, and I'm on the verge of **peaking my game.**"

Alonzo Mourning does not like people invading his space—under the basket, that is. And to ensure privacy, Zo likes to send not-so-friendly reminders to those who try to trespass. Defensively, he greets players with a blocked shot. Offensively, he welcomes them with a left-handed jam. Or a right-handed slam. Either way, each dunk is followed by a nasty scowl that is as imposing as the jam itself. Yes, Alonzo and his dunks intimidate opponents.

"Knowing you're in another player's mind gives you that edge," says Zo. "That's when you're starting to take their confidence away."

Zo thrives on emotion. When he throws one down in the face of an opponent, it only fuels his burning desire to win. And since he is an undersized center at 6–10, Zo has to outwork and outhustle his opponents. But when he receives the ball under the basket, forget about it. Zo and his chiseled body won't be denied.

DID YOU KNOW? ALONZO WAS THE NUMBER-TWO OVERALL PICK IN THE 1992 NBA DRAFT. HE WAS SELECTED AFTER SHAQUILLE O'NEAL.

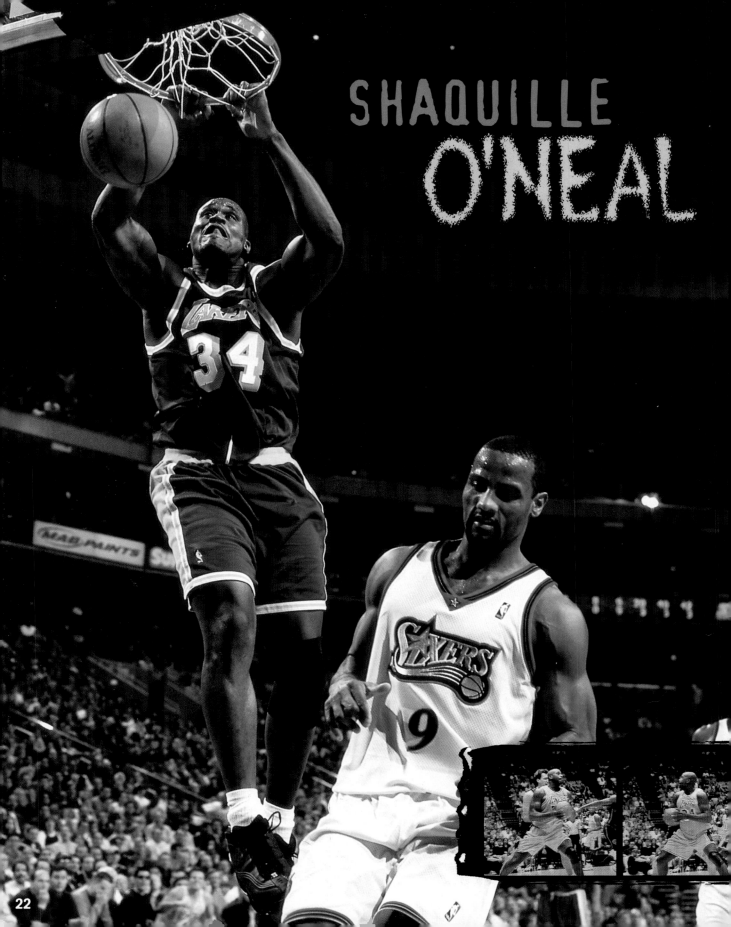

SHAQUILLE O'NEAL

"It feels good to **dunk.** You go out and just **throw it down** with all your **might."**

All talk about Power Dunkers begins with the ultimate Power Dunker—Shaq. The 7–1 315-pound center leads the league in dunks and in embarrassing the opposition. Since he entered the NBA in 1992, Shaq has caused teams nightmares with his thunderous slams and intimidating inside presence. When O'Neal receives the ball under the basket, look out! Or, when he dribbles coast to coast, you better get out of the way. Imagine a locomotive coming at you at full speed. That's what it would be like standing in front of him.

"Dunking makes you feel like you're the strongest man in the world," says O'Neal, who clearly has fun playing basketball.

Some of Shaq's critics think that all he can do is dunk and that's not true. Shaq has developed an all-around game. But when you can jam as well as Shaq and nobody can stop you, wouldn't you throw it down with regularity? And smile while you're doing it?

DID YOU KNOW? SHAQ WAS RECOGNIZED AS ONE OF THE 50 GREATEST PLAYERS IN NBA HISTORY AFTER ONLY FOUR SEASONS IN THE LEAGUE. TALK ABOUT SUDDEN IMPACT!

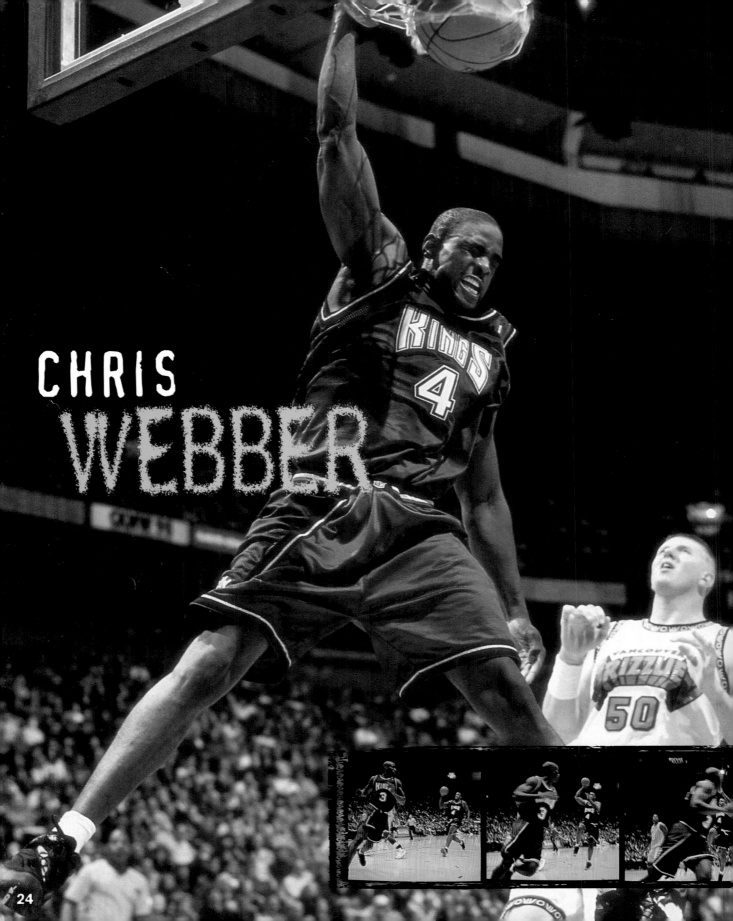

CHRIS
WEBBER

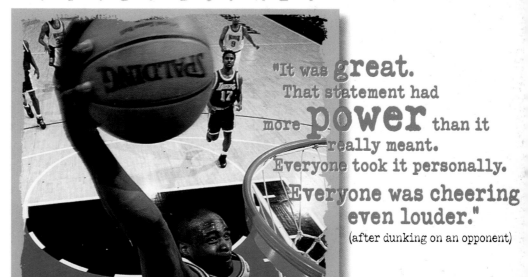

"It was **great.** That statement had more **power** than it really meant. Everyone took it personally. **Everyone was cheering even louder."**

(after dunking on an opponent)

Chris Webber is a flamboyant Power Dunker. During the course of a game, C.Webb will unleash a variety of rim-rocking jams that cause fans to jump out of their seats. First, there's the alley-oop slam. He and his Sacramento King teammate Jason Williams have perfected it. Williams will lead the Kings' fast break and lob the ball to a sprinting C.Webb, who snatches it out of midair with one of his huge hands and brings down the house with a monstrous jam.

Then there's the reverse dunk. C.Webb will drive the baseline and in one big swoop, unload an ultra-quick, wraparound jam. His opponent never had a chance. Finally, there's the coast-to-coast dunk. C.Webb will grab a rebound on the defensive end, dribble the ball the length of the court, and give himself a behind-the-back, wraparound pass before slamming it home. Ask Charles Barkley; he experienced it firsthand.

With C.Webb's combination of size, strength and athleticism, it's better to be an observer than on the receiving end of each dunk. After all, who likes to be embarrassed on national TV?

DID YOU KNOW? CHRIS COLLECTS SIGNED HISTORICAL DOCUMENTS OF PROMINENT AFRICAN-AMERICANS, INCLUDING ITEMS FROM MARTIN LUTHER KING, JR., AND FREDERICK DOUGLASS.

THE DUNKING HALL OF FAME

"I loved the fact that **no one** could really block my shot because I jumped so **high** that there was **nothing** nobody could do."

WILT CHAMBERLAIN

They are the dunking pioneers. Wilt Chamberlain. Elgin Baylor. Gus Johnson. Connie Hawkins. Dr. J. David Thompson. Players who took the game high above the rim and elevated the dunk to new heights. They rocked the basketball establishment with a mixture of powerful and acrobatic jams that forever changed the game.

Prior to the 1960s, the dunk wasn't accepted because it was perceived as the ultimate insult. A sure sign of disrespect. If a player tried to dunk, his opponent would try to take his legs out. Not fun.

All that began to change when Wilt Chamberlain, the massive 7-1 center, who dunked with regularity at the University of Kansas, brought the jam to the NBA. Wilt simply overmatched the opposition with his inside dominance. More dunkers began to emerge, players such as Elgin Baylor and Gus Johnson. Connie Hawkins, a tremendous leaper, added his signature to the dunk with a stylish flair.

Yet the man they call Dr. J raised the bar and brought the dunk to a whole new art form. His moves to the hoop were spectacular yet they had the unrefined quality of a pick-up game. With his enormous hands and long fingers, Julius Erving held the ball like a grapefruit, wielding it in any direction he chose before throwing it down.

He dunked from the free throw line and he dunked from under the glass. He dunked from everywhere. He influenced a generation of dunkers, including Dominique Wilkins and Michael Jordan, and is considered one of the greatest dunkers of all time, if not the greatest.

Here's a look at some of the dunking pioneers in action as well as some of this era's more celebrated aerial acrobats.

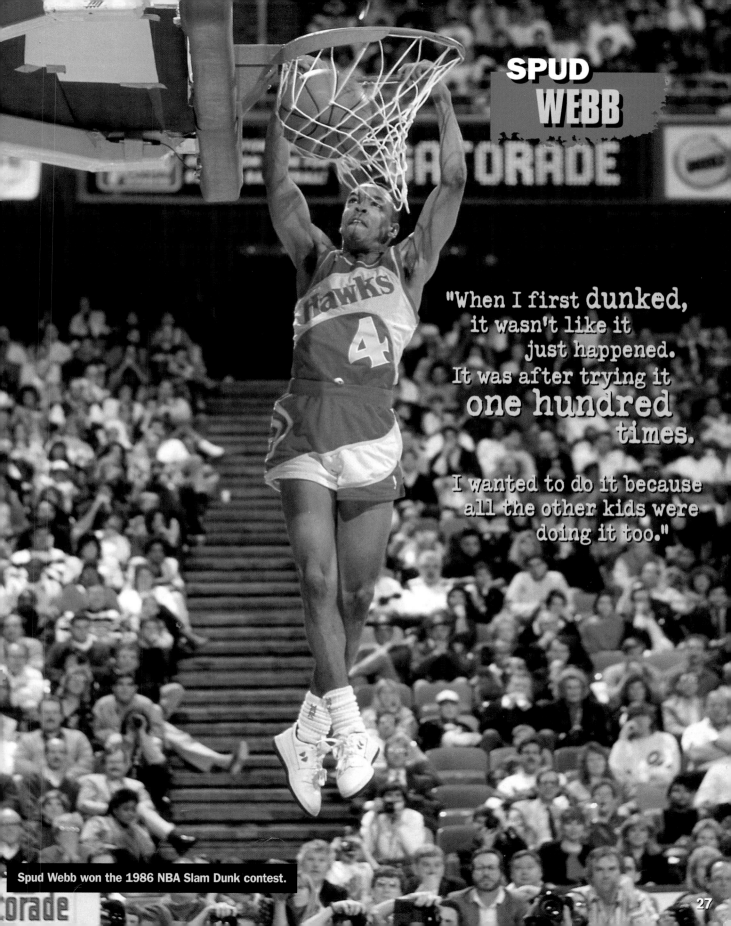

SPUD WEBB

"When I first **dunked**, it wasn't like it just happened. It was after trying it **one hundred** times.

I wanted to do it because all the other kids were doing it too."

Spud Webb won the 1986 NBA Slam Dunk contest.

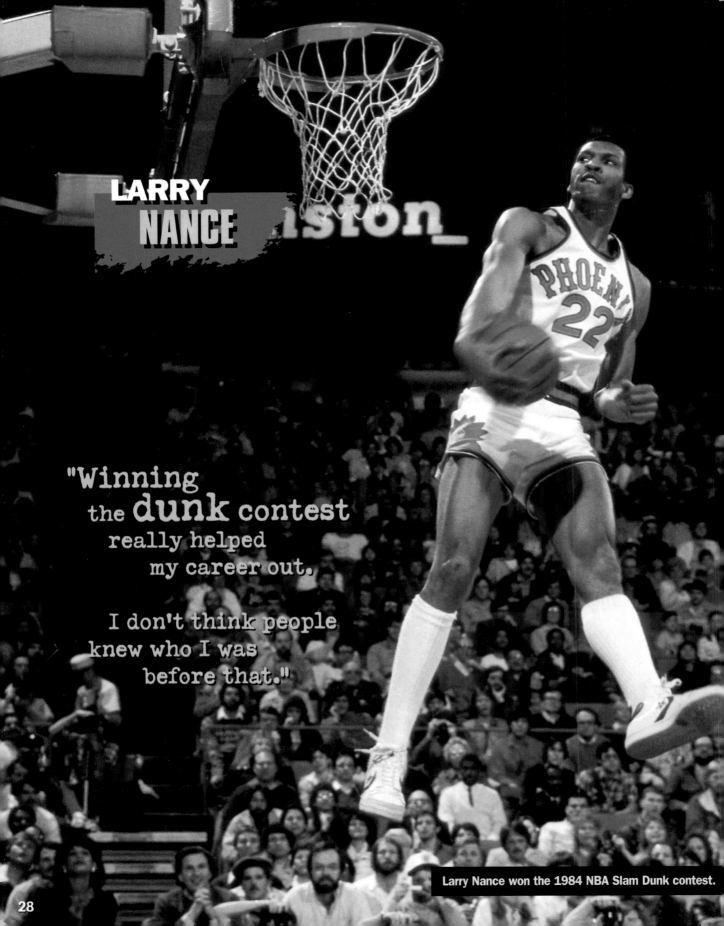

LARRY
NANCE

"Winning
the **dunk** contest
really helped
my career out.

I don't think people
knew who I was
before that."

Larry Nance won the 1984 NBA Slam Dunk contest.

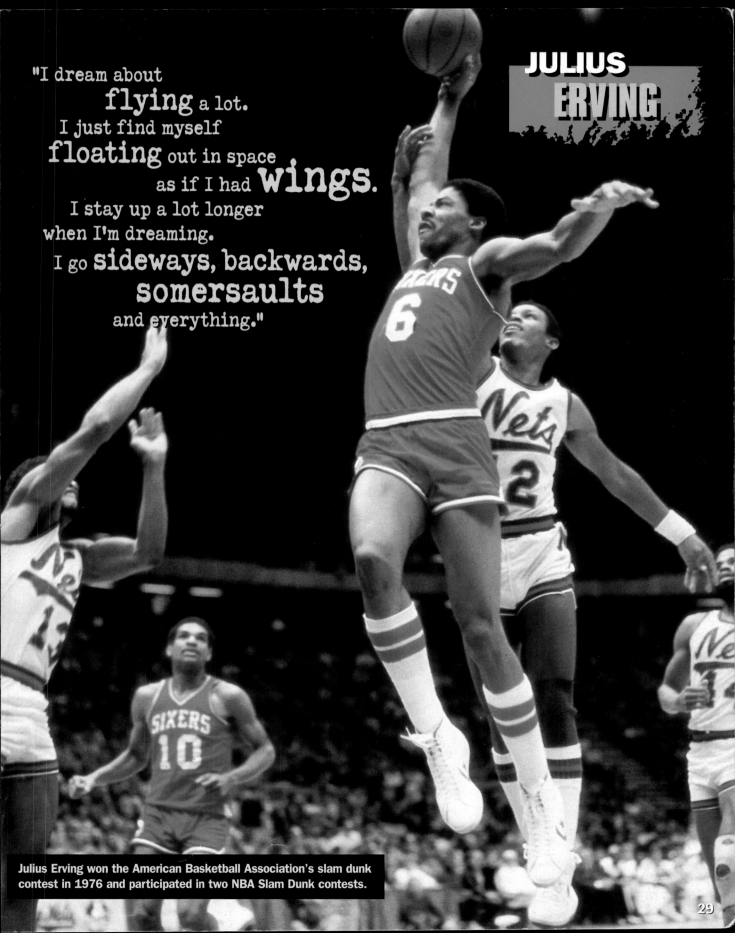

"I dream about **flying** a lot. I just find myself **floating** out in space as if I had **wings.** I stay up a lot longer when I'm dreaming. I go **sideways, backwards, somersaults** and everything."

Julius Erving won the American Basketball Association's slam dunk contest in 1976 and participated in two NBA Slam Dunk contests.

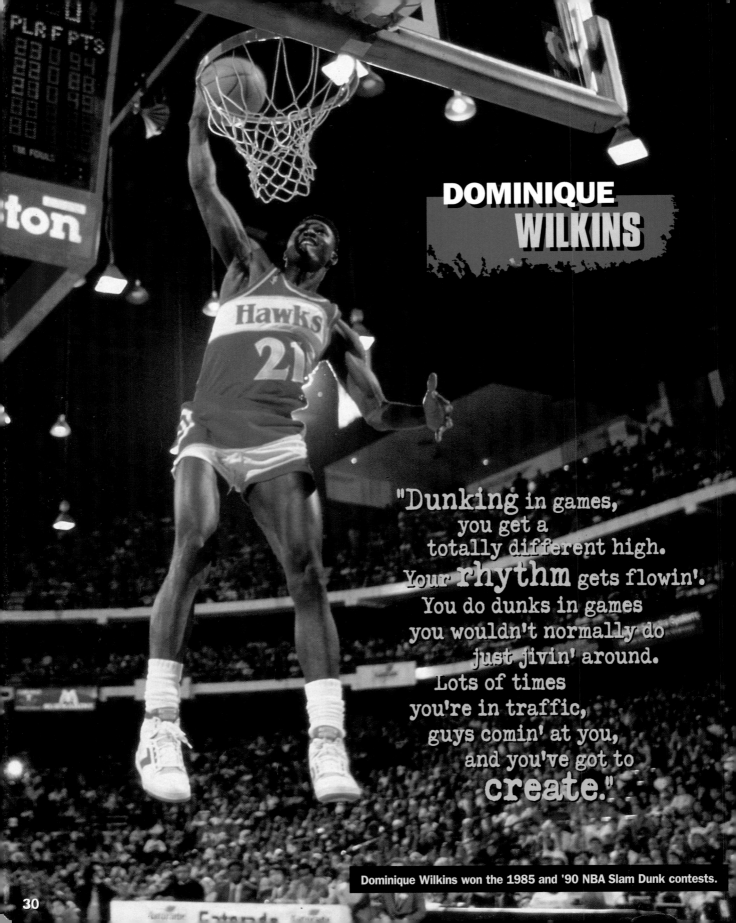

DOMINIQUE
WILKINS

"**Dunking** in games,
you get a
totally different high.
Your **rhythm** gets flowin'.
You do dunks in games
you wouldn't normally do
just jivin' around.
Lots of times
you're in traffic,
guys comin' at you,
and you've got to
create."

Dominique Wilkins won the 1985 and '90 NBA Slam Dunk contests.

CLYDE DREXLER

"Nobody
wants to get into
the **highlights**
that way.

No one wants
to be the
dunkee."

Clyde Drexler participated in five NBA Slam Dunk
contests and twice finished in the top three.

MICHAEL
JORDAN

"I always spread my legs when I jump high, like on my Rock-a-baby, and it seems like I've opened a parachute, like, that slowly brings me back to the floor."

Michael Jordan won the 1987 and '88 NBA Slam Dunk contests.